Pyramid Scheme

Joyce Miller

BookLeaf Publishing

Presentation by *BookLeaf Publishing*

Web: www.bookleafpub.com

E-mail: info@bookleafpub.com

ISBN: 9789357441070

First edition 2023

DEDICATION

Dedicated to Jay Miller and Kay Miller

Soulmites

I do not spite
the humble mite.
The mite deserves not
such a plight.

Mite plays a part
—though small and slight—
no less essential,
no less a fight.

Mite seeks, as I,
to sleep at night.
Mite earns no jeers,
nor jests, nor spite
from I—no worse nor be'er than mite.

Mite wears a beanie, just as I.
Mite is not mine to mock or try.
Mite eats my skin cells when they die.
Know nothing of mite's mysteries I.

Mitey are we.

Die Hard iii

i. Compersion

Ocean floor
Lay I

Kate Winslet
Lies too

The door
Holds two

ii. Cells

There was a jail.
There was a tree.
And from the cell
It could be seen
(Through a tiny crack
where the paint was chipped
on the window painted black)

All the tree could do was grow
All the jail could do was know

Then one day lightning struck

The tree said it's my time
And fell
And crushed the roof of the jail.
And crushed the roof of the jail.

iii. Yoncé’s Inferno

My shine gleams
Nowell screams
attacks
her reflection
image cracks

she engulfed
in my light
(black)
Hole (sun won’t you come)
In (and wash away the rain)
One…

The first ring of hell
as Dante said
Is a feather-weight boxer
With a mallet-head
shadows for hands
a bird that sings
In his heart
When it dies
We suffocate

The second ring
Yoncé is singing
about commitment
regretful transgressions
continuous
monogamous
satanic orgy
One demon
Seven heads

The third ring
Is a buzz
Bee stripes
Yellow black
bee guts
compartmentalizations
And you are inside of them
Jonah and the Bee
too obscure to capture
either audience

The fourth ring of hell
Is clear as a bell
Singing Wineglass
Daily Practice
get it right

sing in unison

with the universe
move the sound
With heaven and hell
With love and hate
With god and devil
not early not late
you broke it

The fifth ring of hell
no edges
no breeze on your face
molecules and you
have no momentum
no memory of parting
you among them
friends at last

The sixth ring of hell
a hundred rings
In ways
That equal death

insight
steals your memory
Your advantage
Your life
significance
Smoothed out of you

The seventh ring of hell
of keys
a door
Down a chute

Your favorite film
The ship crashes
The ring breaks
The sand buries

Finally Ring 8…
of Hell

A theater in the round
High School Production: All's Well that Ends
Well
unwell
unending

audience rotates with actor
we play every role
we get older
eat
shit
die
fuck
birth

Onstage

Land, Sea, Air

I. the radicalization of an octopus

the old bloat
in the old moat
circles round the castle
in her old boat
crying scape goat
slogan totes
for the cold war
compote
for the coal warm
stomped oats
boot wrote
gone gloat
circles round the castle
in her old boat
every day she feeds the sharks
the same oats

fur coats
love notes
all on me will the sun dote
all on me will the sun dote

steal my seat

what to eat
killed me twice
books for mice

through the hole
in the sink
dip those arms
in angel ink

JÖYCE
ECYÖJ

II. Sunbreak

bjcmllr

the sun presents for me
on cold wet stone
i follow rules to see
how they behave
some bright green chains
so see how i'm alone
i am alone
it's an awk u pay shone

you move a chain
and into the garden
up the stairs
on the triangular lawn

into the sky
Alum Inum
a child

bag lunch
pic nic
curb your dog
curb your dog

the ground is not so easy
study rules
tobreakthemwhenitcounts

III. There is no “I” in “L berat on”

u is silent:

m ch 's facade. younger sisters build by the brick. new lease on life. good luck getting that security deposit back. floating interest. simple greed and hatred through the scaffolding. in her floral shapes of murder rose ur doubts.

stringy pummeled sprouts, they detect themselves, in horror, the only living movement. sole heir: excruciating growth, unseen size.

dead witch with sunflower seeds in her pocket.

square crush of institution on gentleness.
excellent copy, exhausting methods. geometric
cruelty flattened from an angle.

there is tots no way, no way the violence of her
hacking into my fb since 2014.

in my too many jokes & hyperarticulate, it's the
babbling of a ruined child.

her abuse of me abandoned in my arms.
keyboard—the better to eat me with. chalking it
up to i can't "just dance" she got her two friends
2 stalk me 2 yoga class & stingray my mat.

violate m ch critiqued her victims for only
writing shitty survivor poetry now.

from a new city in a hat that reads "get out of
my city"

love gasps for life and a new word will our
crawling escape through m ch 's dead brick
never end.

Mark Zuckerberg beckoned into his
crowdsourced dorm room insecurity nightmare
world and we followed willingly

I mean bitch as a character trait and not in a derogatory way against my gender

A bitch died.
In with the rain,
Out with the tide.
A heart lied.
Better to know,
Better to try.
Now we're tied.
The starter ends
Sometime.
I cried.
A bitch runs deep.
A bitch runs wide.

My Work Is Done

1. I have felt love
2. I told the truth
3. I wrote your garbage
4. Into sun
5. I sang the praises
6. Of this life
7. I have felt love
8. My work is done.

9. I asked some questions
10. Mostly fake
11. I never know
12. How much to take
13. I didn't come
14. For friends or fun
15. I have felt love
16. My work is done.

JUST CHECKING TO SEE WHETHER OR NOT YOU HAVE A BODY DOUBLE

Hey,

I know we agreed to go No Contact and, honestly, it's been for the best. Since our time apart, I've grown. I finally accept that the timing just wasn't right for us. I just want to know one thing:

When you passed me on the street without saying anything, was that really you, or was it a body double wearing a replica mask of your face?

Numerous factors go into a relationship. Love is a volatile emotional state that reveals it's endurance over time. Even when love is engineered by a highly trained, deep cover honeytrap operative for the purpose of a clandestine intelligence mission, relationships take work and compatibility.

This is not an excuse to break No Contact, but rather a quest for personal growth. Knowing whether it was you I saw, or a body double wearing a moulded silicone duplicate of your face, will teach me a lot about myself.

This is not only about my happiness. Regardless of our history, I still care about you as a friend. If there is a body double wearing a synthetic duplicate of your face out there, I think it's something you should also know.

I find myself at a loss and left to wonder:

1.) Whether you have multiple body doubles.

and

2.) Whether I was interacting with a body double instead of you at any point during our relationship.

I am therefore forced to re-examine our entire narrative, and what it means if the person with whom I felt such a strong connection was sometimes you and sometimes your body double. It begs the question: if you were able to clone your own face, were you also able to clone mine? Once that trust is broken, you can never get it back.

If we are right for each other, shouldn't I be able to accept that you occasionally need to substitute yourself with another person disguised in a prosthetic rendering of your face? Perhaps I distanced myself from you during the times when I intuited you weren't yourself, but a masked body double, because I knew it meant that we were moving to the next level and got panicked by the intimacy.

They say love asks no questions, but this is more of a general concern. If you could reply with a simple "Yes," to confirm that it was really you I saw, and not a specialized operative who spent five hours in a make-up chair applying facial prosthesis, I will finally be able to move on.

I considered writing this email without actually sending it, as a healing exercise, but concluded that the exchange of information is crucial in this case. It may also be necessary to inform the person your body double was meeting for dinner, in case they are in danger.

I contacted all your social media accounts due to the time-sensitive nature of this message. If none of this is your doing, and someone has grafted your face onto theirs without your consent, then I apologize for the accusatory tone of this email, and will do everything I can to help you.

I understand if you prefer not to respond. Except that I'll be left to grapple on my own with the uncertainty of whether or not that was you who ignored me, or a body double wearing a replica mask of your face—a face that I once believed to be attached to a person that I once believed myself to be attached to.

I know you can't fix the issues that I need to work on, but not letting me know the times in our relationship when it was your body double instead of you feels unfair to me.

Please think this over and consider that your response will relieve me of a huge burden. If I'm lucky enough to meet someone special again in the future, I am the one who has to wonder whether they are who they say they are, or just a mask.

Statue 28

28 is the lifespan of the soul.
After that point, you're only getting old.
A person can last just about so long,
Then order, or corruption, pulls you down.

And how I love,
How I love,
How I love
To wear the crown.

The golden life is hot and then it cools.
Leave mother, fall in love, and go to school.
The metal burns and kills and keeps the shape
Of all who died inside without escape.

But how I loved,
How I loved,
How I loved,
How I loved.

My Cult

I ask if being at total cause over matter, energy, space, and time means being able to make pizza appear with your mind, and the text does not rule it out. I ask if it is possible to be temporarily attracted to the same sex during moments of aberration, and the text does not rule it out. In self-help cults, you pay to unlock your potential. In Karma cults, you pay to learn that you are right where you need to be.

I give my class presentation on the tools to overcome any obstacle and free mankind from suffering. The other students say it is a cult, so I say being called a cult makes my religion even cooler. I suspect my friends only try to rescue me for college essay material, because after their kindness fails, they begin mocking me–especially Ariana. Our calculus teacher announces that I scored the highest. Ariana demands to know: How? My secret is the learning technique invented by my cult, I inform her. Privately, I beg the teacher not to announce my score again.

Ariana leaves our school to accelerate her academics, and invites me to the homeschool dance in someone's strobe-lit dining room. A tall boy of seventeen, with hair down to his butt, grazes the flesh above the waistband of my jeans with his fingers as we slow-dance. For the fast songs, he pockets his hands, and flings his feet in a Cobainian polka. I am introduced to Synthesia, and sense the other girls silently praying that she does not become famous.

The oddness cited in homeschoolers, I notice, is the oddness cited in kids from my cult: distinct personalities, not homogenized by shared impenetrability to school faculty. I bypass adolescence because I am an adult, only in a smaller body. I prefer a childhood lost to this precocity over one gained in the hierarchy that awaits.

With maturity I can tell she copied from someone's mom, Synthesia bids me,"Goodnight! I hope you will return and see us again!" It used to be that a movie star was a mesmerist who escapes demons by attracting men with cameras. Today, one requires charisma that can survive in a petri dish and is only visible under a microscope.

My parents are losing their house, and I still have no agent. Over the phone, Ariana tells me Synthesia is a washed up TV starlet. In my cult, any negativity towards an artist is a sign of evil. Ariana suggests Synthesia and I become Facebook friends, surely to expose our mutual pettiness, but I have none, because I know the universe has a plan for me.

Ariana is devastated to find leaked celebrity nudes of Synthesia in her boyfriend's Google history, so I look them up in secret. I search Synthesia on Facebook for glimmers of scandal, but she has unfriended me. The universe is probably protecting me, I think, until an article mentions Synthesia, draped across the furniture at a meditation group hosted by a celebrated filmmaker, and I wonder, What if the universe is protecting her more than me? For the first time, I feel envious.

I find out, the hard way, that my cult stalks and hacks you when you leave. Not without satisfaction, I find a chapter about Synthesia's meditation group in my copy of Recovery from Cults. It says that they believe you can make Mexican food appear with your mind, but they don't have religious tax status like my cult–only an accredited university. Advertisements for their film program float down my Facebook feed. Students stranded in Florida are willing themselves to levitate until someone buys their screenplay. At least I joined my cult for spiritual growth, I think, and realize how small-minded I have become since leaving.

I tell the registrar I have returned to make amends. The most dedicated are still here, putting off their acting careers until the next lifetime, so that there can be a next lifetime. How I took them for granted. How the media lies. "My father is experiencing body death," I say. "He has refused to leave the bathtub for three days. My mother only told me now." I glow in the embrace of reassuring truths that murmur from the speakers, in this Church, pristine with sanity, high above a city ruled by madmen and merchants of chaos. On a television monitor, Synthesia shares her success story: She has just been cast in a spy thriller starring our most famous actor.

The Riddle

Bobby and Karen lay dead on the floor,
the horses stampeded. The Lord
of the manner demanded to know
what had happened. The servants
assured him they didn't hear
anything over the sound of the races,
and found in their places
a little spilled water
and broken glass.

Two lost souls,
one fish bowl,
The two were bound to fight.
Year after year, we waited
to see what would happen.

The Master just sighed,
and quietly turned to the window.
What happened?

The Willis

Tonight meet me up in the fresh dirt mound.

Ask for the queen of the underground.

So many sunken sleeps, but you choose mine.

You want to dance, I dance you till you die.

Where are they disposed for the pleasure of us girls?

We do not know. We fade in gleaming twirls.

Feet dance on me, the dirt shakes down within—

A measured spirit, screaming for my twin.

Now dancing hollow, dancing for the night

In earthless pleasure, cannot stop for life.

So many sunken sleeps, but you choose mine,

To dance until the sunlight on the pine.

I dance for greed that others bear with grace,

For pity there's no pity on my face.

Fair ones who just arrived and cause no harm,

Will only serve as compost for the farm.

“The ones I’ve loved have either left or died.

Will no one stay and dance with me?” I cried.

A soul enslaved to wicked indifference,

I never seem to have a moments rest.

Morning always begins the same:

Dancing in an endless night

… Inspired by the biography of Nureyev.

I Tried

I.
I tried,
But you didn't hear.
I fight,
But can't stand in the light.
I tried,
But I can't crack it open,
All that glitters is broken.
I tried,
When they called your name,
But they did not call mine.

II.
I am the suspension
And the washed up shore
I am the cliff,
The sea,
The drop between.

We make our own punishment
We make our own rewards
In the foam,
A thousand dances twirl,
The waves pearl Giant’s neck.

Giant tells us
There is no god
Only we matter
And are god
Tell me
Who has made me
Matter
So that I may know
Who to worship.

III.
But how will I recognize you
In the next life
How do I recognize you
In the lives before?

In defiance of memory's betrayal, a coup d'etat
of unseen ecosystems,
Through the smoke of language, an insurrection
of unworded thought,
As I recognize you now,
A bright light shattering the night,
Regardless of all the reasons not to.

A Dress for the Funeral

It is perfectly legal to start planning a memorial gala for someone 63 years in advance of her projected death-of-natural-causes-after-a-long-fulfilling-life-sur rounded-by-loved-ones, as a healing ritual for forgiveness.

Today I learned to forgive someone. Nowell will be dead in 63 years if she dies at an even 100. I called and booked the funeral parlor for Sunday, April 20, 2085, at my expense.

I have sent the invitations to her friends and family, and all our mutual acquaintances, and asked everyone for their dietary restrictions.

I am so excited and want us all to be part of planning the big day when we will celebrate Nowell's life.

Black orchids, a cake from Momofuku, and pictures of her face that I've photoshopped onto the bodies of Victorian men in powdered wigs as a nod to her royal lineage and property accumulation. Nowell's family probably owned slaves on both sides, and it showed.

Though Nowell is happily alive and well, and will be for some time, I practice speaking of her strictly in the past tense because I want my speech to be flawless.

I have started a GoFundMe to order a black Vivienne Westwood gown for myself when I host.

I have reached out to each guest, requesting a description of their favorite memories with Nowell.

Everything I'm doing for Nowell is a kindness I am happy to give, reveling in the thought of how wonderful she will look in her casket when she is dead—dead, of course, at one hundred, from natural causes, having lived a long, fulfilling life.

One possibility for the memorial is hooking the corpse up to a motorized cable system so that Nowell can dance. She loved to dance.

I know what you are thinking—it is presumptuous of me to imagine I will be alive long enough to follow through and foot the bill for this memorial I have been planning. Not to worry—Nowell was much older than I am. I consider it paying my dues to the elders.

Another thing I have managed to put together is a grave plot for Nowell. I went ahead and took the initiative to pick a headstone. I bought it at a discount because it was pre-carved for whoever returned it. They told me "Gerald" is very easy for the memorial mason to convert to "Nowell," and that the dates can get redone once they are final.

We could host a gravedig where everyone pays five dollars to shovel a bucket of dirt and drink free beer from that local brewery in Brooklyn that Nowell liked.

We can practice what we will say as the coffin is lowered into the ground, and audition early career ministers who can commit to an event that far in advance.

We should allow underrepresented artists a chance to perform at the memorial. Nowell was a champion of the arts. It is not necessary for Nowell to attend rehearsals. A stand-in will suffice. I've already set up the Facebook Event Invite. Please RSVP. It is called "Quite the Undertaking."

Somewhere along the way, as I plan this great event to show my good will and that I only wish Nowell a long and happy life to be celebrated after her passing, you and I try to maintain the appropriate distance.

Somewhere between purple satin coffin interior swatches and cereal milk cake tastings, the ice is broken and you look at me with a certain timidity and we start talking.

It difficult, but it is necessary, and it is good—because Nowell meant so much to both of us. The fact that Noelle died 63 years from now, of natural causes, surrounded by loved ones, only makes us feel a sense of immediacy to express our true feelings—because she would have wanted us both to be happy.

At one of the many death bed rehearsals over the next several decades, Nowell's stand-in gazed out at us and, with kindly tears in her wise old eyes, filled with a light and wisdom possessed only by those who will soon cross over, she said, "You two are meant to be together."

At the end of the night, you offer to help clean up after the party. "I just miss her so much," we both sob, collapsing into each other's arms. Then, the energy shifts to unmistakable passion, and even though we both think it's so wrong, everything feels so right between us, and we can't deny ourselves.

We are both trying to do what is right. Love happens when you least expect.

Giving Up On Humanity

Sometimes I stay home,
To Practice clapping,
Pretending to smile,
At things I don't like.

Smiling and nodding.
Laughing and cheering.
For the overall good.
There are things that you do.

Am I insane to dislike what most people like?
This is what they prefer to believe.
That there is something wrong with me, and
right with them.
And it is much safer for me to let them.

The Fingermaid’s Tale

The Fingermaid's Tale
Could fit
On the fingermaid's nail.

On Christmas
She fines up her nail bonnet
With a red rhinestone

Her mouth and eyes
Are drawn in pen
She cannot speak

Her words can only
Be read on the page,
Or heard in the mind,
As you lock eyes
With the fingermaid.

You see yourself
Come alive in the fingermaid
And the two of you are joined forever

She says

Do not be afraid, come follow,

I am the shell of my former self,
The oyster of my present self,
And the pearl of my future self,
As well as the ocean,
And the world.
I am Ruby, the fingermaid from The
Fingermaid's Tale and I am all things.

And then she sings, in a great and unexpected voice that you are only able to listen to in your head, and that no one else can hear:

My name is Ruby
I am all the time
In your mind
Don't wait to find
The joy inside
I am alive
I am kind

For I am Ruby
Deep within a place
That's so safe
While you face
The human race
Leave no trace
Just keep pace

I'm Ruby

I'll show you the way
If you say
I hear you pray
Yes you may
Don't have to stay
There is a new day

Ruby
I'll guide you through
It's so new
I am true
And I flew
Back to you
The only thing to do

Ruby
There was so much
I couldn't touch
And I blush
For there's such
Consciousness
But I will be your crutch

Ruby
Lift up your eyes
In surprise
At the size
Of who lies
And who tries

Hear the cries

Oh I am Ruby
Dancing all alone
I have shone
I have grown
And I’ve shown
It is better to have flown
And lived your life on a loan

For here is Ruby
I’m the tiny truth
That removes
All the pain of your youth
Not a thing was uncouth
Nail and tooth
Floor to roof
Ruby

Mantras

I.
Choose love
Not fear

Even when it's bad
The world is so good
Always love

Always love

Always love

Leap

And the net will appear

II.
Me=Motorcycle Diaries
Ur Gf=Motorcycle Diarrhea

Me=Shakespeare
Ur Gf=Cape Fear

Me=Elizabeth Taylor

Ur Gf=Elizabeth Failure

After extensive therapy
I have discovered
I don't need to heal
Or realize that I am enough
Or stop the negative self talk
Or learn to love myself first
Or learn forgiveness
I just need motherfuckers to give me back my money.

Though I lack these upper middle class protections, I am grateful that:

It is perfectly legal to entertain an extensive imagined relationship with a muse who has played you, ghosted you, and tried to lock you out of upward mobility.

The Yoga Teacher: For today's practice, give yourself the mantra "I am enough. I deserve to be loved."

Me: Well it's not like I had any doubt until you said it that way.

III.
VIDEOSCAPE 3/10

YOU MUST BE OPEN
YOU MUST NOT BE RIGID
YOU MUST NOT REQUIRE
THE NEARNESS OF
YOUR OWN DEATH
TO FEEL ALIVE
FOR MORTALITY IS
ALL AROUND US
OR IS IT
COME LET US FEAST
ON SUGAR FREE ENERGY DRINKS
BODEGA COFFEE AND SANDWICHES
UNNATURALLY COLORED SNACK CHIPS
O TELL ME, WHERE IS MY JOY,
MY GLAMOUR MY YOUTH

Reticular Activation System

I told myself,
"If I get it in the wastepaper basket,
my love is equally returned,"
And without question, every time, I did.

Then, a jealous rival made me miss.
The net appeared,
And it was made of barbed wire.
Yet, as my seventh and final year of bad luck
comes to a close:

I recall, we both knew,
Their wedding was our wedding.
I ate only fresh apples the morning after,
Until they coursed through my system.

I never stole anyone's love,
And nobody ever stole mine.

Of Rhythm

I. We dance parallel dances,
And think parallel thoughts,
Taking parallel chances,
Moving on when we ought.

We each play our own story in our mind,
Thinking we all see the world the same,
Does the one who stops to find the answer,
Stop their dancing, and so lose the game?

II. I must take care to never become a vagabond.
Only the rich may wander and then return unscathed.
I am too pretty. The others will lure me into the field,
Away from the herd, and I will become their prey.

The rich man's child conceals their favors from an early age—
They learned in the schoolyard to master me under the guise of play,
Pretending that I am their equal until the moment it is too late—

Pretended that I was their equal until I could not escape.

III. When you rhyme,
It only means
That half your dreams
Cannot keep time.

The cherished half
Has come in vogue—
The other, silent,
Has gone rogue.

Worship Junkie

I. Jesus was a heretic
For telling Lady Grey
The water all had meds in it,
Was time to run away.

They sailed for many moons,
A quarter and a day,
But couldn't seem to make the trip,
Before time washed away.

Annie was a movie star,
Or so she had been told,
And made her way to the factory,
Where words are bought and sold.

She tried to make a difference,
Before the empire fell.
The ladies all applauded her,
The dead, they wished her well.

The ship was still a sinking,
And the tires had been slashed.
The statues just sat thinking,
That the shuttle soon would crash.

They took a stand,
And hand in hand,
They did not give a damn,
They took their place in the history of man.

Fancy was a happy girl,
No one could do her harm.
Dancing on the beach,
She took her old gentleman's arm.

The riot calls and golden balls
All fell upon the town,
And she knew that she would greet them
In a brand new wedding gown.

The people came to flood the wall,
And I was waving down
A thousand miles and bathroom stalls,
But no one was around.

Did you mark the call,
And did you all across the nation?
It just takes one to fall in love,
And kill the operation.

II. She's the kind of man you meet,
And know that you just killed a prophet,
With eyes you cannot bear to see,
Unless you brought an offering.

Then the band resumes,
And you work the room,
For the body has been taught.

So you let her go,
And they smile and know,
We sleep another knot.

Get dead, stay dead,
It feels so good,
When spirit leaves the body.

Get in my head,
I wish you would,
Like it's a Mazzerati.

She's the kind of man you meet,
When you're walking down the street,
And accuse of casting spells,
So instead you wish her well.

Now you know what hope can do,
And you know you see the light,
But there's darkness over there,
And there's comfort in the night.

You haven't felt the river swell,
You haven't heard the lies they tell,
She is standing next to you,
Asking if you see it too.

But you leave her at the train,
And you promise you'll return,
With the holy revelations,
When the fire has ceased to burn.

III. The Little Bird

A little bird came down one day,
And landed by my side,
And pulled my secrets from me,
With the follow of my eye.

'Til follow her away I did,
Now every day I cry:
I cannot hate the little bird
Who made me see the sky.

Thinspo

I. Care Instructions

Cut like a flower,
Put in a vase.
When the water runs dry,
Blame for escape.

Flowers can
not reroot
I live by
my pollen
The insects
who carry

Save the leaf that fell from my stem
As a memory.
Be gentle to the bees,
They will not report us.

II. May the winter treat you well

May the winter treat you well
And time will tell
But if the clock is wrong I watch the oceans
swell

The earth still moves beneath them and the sun
Can accurately cast when day is done

Nostradamus made his charts
As we all do
But the orbit of the planets slowly staggered out
of line
Which means that what we see and what the
calendar forecasts
May disagree on what is meant to last

But life is never meant to last and life is not long
It's usually the same repeated daily
And if you happen to be on the planet
It is unlikely to stop
How almost as unlikely for us to wind up
together on it at the same time.

Love Triangle

I used to be part of a love triangle,
Now I'm just a line,
I guess that makes me straight,
I guess things are gonna be fine.

I used to be part of a love triangle,
Playing in a one man band,
Now the notes ring sour, and every hour,
I'm wishing for the minute hand.

I used to be part of a love triangle,
And friends with a circle and square,
If you know any shapes that are missing a side,
I've got one to spare.

I used to be part of a love triangle,
But the formula was not right,
Somebody broke my protractor,
And sent me out into the night.

www.ingramcontent.com/pod-product-compliance
Lightning Source LLC
Chambersburg PA
CBHW051738130826
49812CB00033B/916
9789357441070